MATHABILITY
Math in the REAL WORLD

Written by **Michael Cain**

Illustrated by **Mary Lou Johnson**

Prufrock Press Inc.
P.O. Box 8813
Waco, TX 76714-8813
Phone: (800) 998-2208
Fax: (800) 240-0333
http://www.prufrock.com

Contents

Construction Malfunction

1.1 **The Founding of the Foundation** 9
    area of a complex polygon, problem solving using formula   step-by-step practice

1.2 **Up Against the Walls** 10
    problem solving using a diagram, perimeter   prompted practice

1.3 **Dry Wall My Wall** 11
    rate and time   independent practice

1.4 **Debating on Painting** 12
    cost of materials, number operations   step-by-step practice

1.5 **Winter Worries** 13
    cost of materials, measurement, using the area formula   prompted practice

1.6 **The White Room** 14
    ratio, area   independent practice

1.7 **Carpeting the Stairs** 15
    measurement conversion, number operations   independent practice

1.8 **Roof over Their Heads** 16
    rate, time, cost   challenge

1.9 **Live Wire** 17
    measurement, number operations, estimation   independent practice

1.10 **Plenty of Pipes** 18
    measurement, number operations, total cost   challenge

Making Ends Meet

2.1 **Figuring Out the Furniture** 20
    real number operations, comparing numbers   step-by-step

2.2 **Checking and Balancing** 21
    real number operations, algebra, comparing numbers   prompted practice

2.3 **Catching the Bus** 22
    rate, time, drawing a diagram, algebra   challenge

2.4 **Dirty Laundry** 23
    fractions, proportion, number relations, algebra   step-by-step

2.5 **More Dirty Laundry** 24
    percent, proportion, determining pertinent information   prompted practice

2.6 **Mall Madness** 25
    discount, percent of decrease   independent practice

2.7 **Ticket to Ride** 26
    schedules, time   independent practice

2.8 **Lots of Lottery Tickets** 27
    probability   challenge

2.9 **Food for Thought** 28
    number operations, percent   independent practice

2.10 **Wear and Tear** 29
    percent of decrease   challenge

A Well Deserved Vacation

3.1 **Fill'er Up** 31
ratio, number operations, problem solving   step-by-step

3.2 **Sandwich Assembly Line** 32
unit prices   prompted practice

3.3 **Car Trouble** 33
time, rate, drawing a diagram   independent practice

3.4 **Repair Scare** 34
rate, unit prices   step-by-step

3.5 **Middle of Nowhere** 35
rate, scale, number conversion   prompted practice

3.6 **Hotel at Last** 36
percent of discount   independent practice

3.7 **Dining Out** 37
number operations, percent   independent practice

3.8 **Amusements at the Park** 38
algebra   challenge

3.9 **Bungle in the Jungle** 39
probability   independent practice

3.10 **Road Side Attraction** 40
similar figures, ratio, proportion   independent practice

Care and Feeding

4.1 **Lost and Found** 42
unit price   step-by-step

4.2 **It's in the Bag** 43
unit price, comparing real numbers   prompted practice

4.3 **Doing the Can Can** 44
unit price, comparing real numbers   independent practice

4.4 **Walking the Dog** 45
measure of central tendency   step-by-step

4.5 **How Big Will It Get?** 46
finding a pattern, making a graph, extrapolating   prompted practice

4.6 **Vet Bills and Budget Chills** 47
percent, number operations   independent practice

4.7 **The Dog Show You Know** 48
permutations, combinations   independent practice

4.8 **Don't Fence Me In** 49
perimeter, measurement, number operations   independent practice

4.9 **Gear Is Here** 50
surface area   challenge

4.10 **How Much Does It Eat** 51
time, rate, unit price, projected cost   challenge

Minding a Business

5.1 Time and Time Again 53
  units of time and labor cost, multi-step problem solving   independent practice

5.2 Laboring Over Cost 54
  creating and applying formulas, using new information   independent practice

5.3 Triangle Tangle 55
  Pythagorean formula, number operations   step-by-step

5.4 Ramp Champ 56
  Pythagorean formula, operations with variables, order of operation   prompted practice

5.5 Dawning of the Awning 57
  transform the Pythagorean formula, operations with variables   independent practice

5.6 Moving Belts and Improving Belts 58
  Pythagorean formula, multi-step problem   challenge

5.7 As the Tire Turns 59
  measurement, circumference, number operations   prompted practice

5.8 Tired of Tires 60
  measurement, circumference formula, completing a chart   independent practice

5.9 Thanks for the Water Tanks 61
  volume of a cylinder   challenge

5.10 Bang for the Banquet 62
  using a table, applying information, multi-step problem solving   independent practice

Home Sweet Home

6.1 Holiday Savings 64
  algebra, interest   step-by-step

6.2 Saving for a Rainy Day 65
  simple interest, algebra   prompted practice

6.3 Stocking Stuffers 66
  real number operations   independent practice

6.4 The Big Bird 67
  time, units of measure conversion   step-by-step

6.5 Bus Fuss 68
  rate, distance, algebra, comparing numbers   prompted practice

6.6 Buses and Trains 69
  schedules, time   independent practice

6.7 Furnishing a Room 70
  algebra, number operations   independent practice

6.8 How Does the Garden Grow? 71
  geometric formulas, number operations   independent practice

6.9 Preparing for Winter 72
  geometric formulas, percent, comparing real numbers   independent practice

6.10 Birthday Celebration 73
  percent, operations with decimals   independent practice

Answers 74

Information for the Instructor

Math for the Real World

Welcome to the world of Clever and Smart. These two characters have a variety of the same real-world experiences that your students will have when they are adults. Through these experiences they will introduce students to many applications for the math processes they learn in school. Join Clever and Smart as they build a house, budget their money, go on vacation, care for a dog, open a business, and run a household.

The situations presented in each problem are realistic circumstances that people encounter on a daily basis. By practicing the mathematics involved in each of these situations, students not only practice important techniques and problem-solving strategies, but they also see practical applications for what they are taught in school. Seeing these common situations gives new meaning to what otherwise might be perceived as inessential knowledge. These problems are the answer to the age-old question, "when are we going to use this stuff?" and are sure to build math abilities.

Four Types of Problems

The problems in *Mathability* are presented in four different formats: step-by-step, prompted practice, independent practice, and challenge.

- The **step-by-step** problems are designed for remediation or introduction to a particular type of problem. Each step of the solution is outlined, with space provided for student to do the calculations and explain the work.

- The **prompted practice** problems include less-specific guidance and space for calculations and explanations of each step in the solution. These can be used as intermediate steps between step-by-step problems and independent work.

- The **independent practice** and **challenge** problems do not give students any guidance in solving the problem. Having worked through the step-by-step and prompted practice, students should have a background that will allow them to solve these problems on their own. The challenge problems are more difficult than the independent practice problems and may be used to challenge your ablest students or to reinforce work students have done with the other three types of problems.

Taken as a whole, the questions cover a wide array of math topics and cover all the major content areas used in standards-based testing. You can use all four formats or only those problems that you feel meet the needs of your students. In a basic or remedial class, you might choose to use only the step-by-step and prompted practice problems. In an advanced math class you would probably skip the first two types of problems and give students the independent practice and challenge problems.

Presentation and Solution

This program is easy to implement. The problems in *Mathability* need very little presentation. The introductory paragraph and the directions give students enough information to tackle the problems. Some of the instructions in the introduction are repeated in the directions, so students who skimmed over the first presentation of what is required will have one more opportunity to zero in on what they must do to.

In all of these problems students are instructed to do the calculations, to explain each step of the problem solving process, and to write their final answer in a complete sentence. The worksheets provide spaces for both calculations and written explanations. These three components of an acceptable solution are aligned with current trends in testing. Your state or school district may or may not stress having students write about the problem solving strategies they use. By explaining each step they use and why they used it, however, students gain a better understanding of the "whys" behind the "hows" of problem solution.

Each chapter presents problems that deal with a particular aspect of real life – raising a pet, owning a business, going on vacation, etc. At the beginning of each chapter is a form that lists each problem in the chapter and has a space for recording grades. If students are working on these units independently the forms can be used to record their work, so both you and the students have a record of their progress. These chapter outlines can also be used to report progress to parents, pinpointing what types of math skills the student has mastered or what skills need additional practice.

Assessment

The assessment of open-ended questions like the ones presented in this book requires some sort of benchmark. The benchmark acts as a guide for assessing proficiency levels. The structure of how the answer is presented can differ widely from student to student, however, certain commonalities do exist. Answers can be viewed as four basic categories: mastery, proficient, nearly proficient, and non-proficient.

- Mastery answers are always clear, fully explained, well-organized, and correct. Since most state standard exams are graded by individuals other than the math instructor, an answer must be understandable by anyone on grade level.

- A proficient answer is always correct, but the explanation may lack clarity. Full sentences are necessary for a mastery level, but often a proficient-level answer will be in phrases and have incorrect grammar and spelling.

- A near-proficient level answer is either a correct answer with no explanation or a correct explanation with a miscalculation.

- A non-proficient answer is neither correct nor explained.

Using these basic guidelines and taking the skill level of your students into consideration, you can adjust your expectations for assessing each problem. As a follow-up it helps to do each problem together after students have worked the problems individually and review the explanations for each step.

Presenting a similar problem on the board a day or two prior to assigning one of these questions gives students a familiarity with the question and its correct answer and will expedite the time needed for assessment.

Get Ready for the Real World

Mathability provides practice in open-ended questions that are used on state and district standards assessment, but more importantly, it gives students practice solving real-world problems. Using this format will give students a background in the different ways math can be used to save money, make decisions, and plan for the best results.

Construction Malfunction

Get out your tape measure and join Clever and Smart as they build a house. This adventure tests their abilities to "hit the nail on the head" and also to figure the costs of materials they will need to complete each project. From the foundation to the roof, there are plenty of ways to use mathematics with this true-to-life project.

	skills	completed	grade
1.1	area of a polygon, problem solving using a formula		
1.2	problem solving using a diagram, perimeter		
1.3	rate and time		
1.4	cost of materials, number operations		
1.5	cost of materials, measurement, using area formula		
1.6	ratio, area		
1.7	measurement conversion, number operations		
1.8	rate, time, cost		
1.9	measurement, number operations, estimation		
1.10	measurement, number operations, cost		

Evaluation of work in this unit

_____

_____

_____

_____

_____

© Prufrock Press Inc. • *Mathability*

1.1 The Founding of the Foundation

Name _____

area of a complex polygon, problem solving using formula
step-by-step practice

20m

15m

10m

15m

5m

5m

Clever and Smart are building a house. They are about to pour the foundation. How much cement should they pour? Clever thinks they need to pour 70 square meters of concrete. Smart thinks that 425 square meters is the correct amount. Who is right?

☞ Directions

Determine which, if either, is the correct amount of concrete. Justify your answer by showing all the steps used. Explain the reason for using each step. Write your final answer in a complete sentence.

1. Divide the shape into two different rectangles. What are the dimensions of the two rectangles?

2. Recall the formula for area of a rectangle. Write the formula.

3. Use the area formula to find the area of both rectangles. What operation did you use?

4. Combine the two answers. The result will be the total area of the foundation.

1.2 Up Against the Walls

problem solving using a diagram, perimeter
prompted practice

Name _____

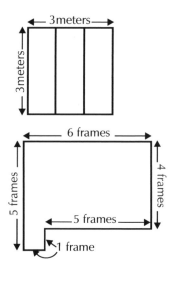

Clever and Smart are building frames for the sides of the house. Each frame will be in the shape of a square. Each frame is 3 meters in length and width. There will be 2 more boards placed in the center one meter apart for support (top diagram). They know how many frames they will need for each side of the house (bottom diagram). They need to know how many boards it will take to make all of the frames.

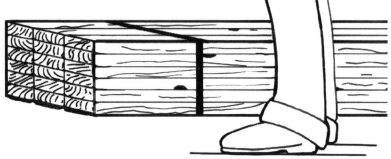

☞ Directions

Determine the number of boards needed to make all the frames. Explain how you got your answer. Explain each step you use.

▸ How many boards are in one frame?

▸ How many frames will be needed for the entire house?

▸ Use the two figures to calculate the total amount of boards.

1.3 Dry Wall My Wall

rate and time
independent practice

Clever and Smart are putting up the dry wall on the inside of the house. Clever can put up a sheet in 7 minutes. It takes Smart 9 minutes to put up one sheet. They have agreed to each put up half the dry wall sheets. There are 74 sheets of dry wall. If Smart does not start to work until Clever has finished the first half of the job, how long will it take to get all of the dry wall sheets put up in the house?

☞ Directions
Determine how long it will take to put up all the dry wall. Convert your answer into hours and round the answer to the nearest hour. Explain each step you use and why.

work area

explanation

_____

_____

_____

_____

_____

_____

_____

_____

_____

_____

_____

_____

_____

_____

_____

_____

_____

1.4 Debating on Painting

cost of materials, number operations
step-by-step practice

Name _____

Clever and Smart are ready to buy paint to paint the house. They need to buy 19 gallons of exterior paint and 15 gallons of interior paint. How much will it cost to paint the house inside and out?

Price List
5-gallon bucket of exterior paint $33.75 each
1-gallon bucket of interior paint $13.50 each

☞ **Directions**
Determine the total cost of the paint. Using complete sentences, explain each step.

1. Determine how many 5-gallon buckets of exterior paint they will need.
   Hint: Any remainders require buying another full bucket.

----

2. Determine how much all the exterior paint will cost.

----

3. Determine the cost of 15 one-gallon buckets of interior paint.

----

4. Combine your two answers to find the total cost of the paint. Label your answer.

1.5 Winter Worries

cost of materials, measurement, using the area formula
prompted practice

Clever and Smart are going to insulate the attic of their house. They need to figure out how much insulation they will need and how much it will cost. Use the diagram to calculate the area of the attic. If insulation costs $15.00 a roll and each roll is 1.5 meters by 3 meters, find the cost of the insulation.

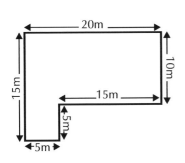

☞ Directions

Determine how much insulation they will need to buy and how much it will cost. Use complete sentences to explain each step you take to solve the problem and the operations you use.

▶ Divide the area into two rectangles and find the area of each rectangle. Add the two areas to find the total area of the attic floor.

_____
_____

▶ Find the area of one roll of insulation.

_____
_____

▶ Divide the area of the attic by the area of the insulation. This is how many rolls of insulation you will need.

_____
_____

▶ Calculate the total cost of the insulation.

_____
_____
_____

1.6 The White Room

ratio, area
independent practice

Clever and Smart are painting their living room white. The original color on the walls is brown. They will have to put 2 coats of paint on the walls to completely cover the old brown paint. Each gallon of paint will cover 200 square feet of wall space. Each gallon of paint costs $23.75. Use the diagrams showing each of the four walls and the placement and size of the window and door to find out how many gallons of white paint they will need and how much the paint will cost.

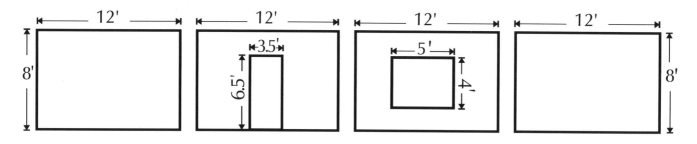

☞ Directions

Determine how much paint they will need to purchase and how much it will cost. Use complete sentences to explain each step you take to solve the problem and the reason for each step.

work area

explanation

_ _

_ _

_ _

_ _

_ _

_ _

_ _

_ _

_ _

_ _

_ _

_ _

1.7 Carpeting the Stairs

measurement conversion, number operations
independent practice

Name _____

Clever and Smart are going to install a carpet on their staircase. The carpet is only sold in yards. Their staircase has 14 steps. They want to carpet both the vertical and horizontal parts of each stair. In addition to the stairs, they want to have a 2.5-foot piece of carpet for both the upstairs landing and the first floor landing. Using the diagram, find how much carpet they need. Round your answer to the nearest yard.

☞ Directions
Determine the length of carpet in yards that they will need for the entire staircase and the landings. Use complete sentences to explain each step you use to solve the problem and the reason for each step.

←—10″—→
8″

work area

explanation

_ _

_ _

_ _

_ _

_ _

_ _

_ _

_ _

_ _

_ _

_ _

_ _

_ _

_ _

_ _

1.8 Roof Over Their Heads

rate, time, cost
challenge

Clever and Smart are going to cover their roof with cedar shingles. Their roof has an area of 2025 square feet. The shingles they want to use come in bundles of 100 square feet and are only sold in full bundles. Each bundle costs $171.95. They will need to hire a trained specialist to help them with the work. The specialist charges a flat fee of $500 plus $25.00 an hour. The specialist can attach one bundle of shingles in 1 hour. The specialist will complete half of the roof. It will take Clever and Smart 2 hours to attach a bundle of shingles. How much will it cost to shingle their roof?

☞ Directions

Determine the total cost to shingle the roof. Include both material cost and labor cost. Use complete sentences to explain each step you use to solve the problem and the reason for each step.

work area

explanation

- -

- -

- -

- -

- -

- -

- -

- -

- -

- -

- -

- -

- -

- -

- -

1.9 Live Wire

measurement, number operations, estimation
independent practice

Name _____

The second floor of Clever and Smart's new house needs to have 3 more electrical outlets installed. Each outlet is a different distance from the circuit breaker box. Outlet A is about 72 feet away. Outlet B is about 87 feet away. Outlet C is about 102 feet away. The wire needed is sold in 30-yard boxes. Each box of wire costs $14.95. Estimate the cost of the wire to connect all three outlets.

☞ Directions

Using estimation, determine the total cost of the wire needed for all 3 outlets. Remember wire is sold in complete boxes, not as pieces. Use complete sentences to explain each step you use to solve the problem and the reason for each step.

work area

explanation

_____
_____
_____
_____
_____
_____
_____
_____
_____
_____
_____
_____
_____
_____
_____

1.10 Plenty of Pipes

measurement, number operations, total cost
challenge

To install all the plumbing in the house, Clever and Smart will need a variety of supplies. Use the chart to help calculate the cost of all the plumbing supplies they will need.

	amount needed	price
copper tubing	675 feet	$34.32 in a 15-yard roll
copper elbow joints	45	$1.34 each
copper tee joints	35	$2.75 each
copper 45° joints	45	76¢ each
shut off values	10	$5.67 each

☞ Directions

Determine the total cost to purchase all the plumbing supplies. Use complete sentences to explain each step you use to solve the problem and the reason for each step.

work area   explanation

18

Making Ends Meet

Clever and Smart are living on their own and discovering all the trials of balancing their income and expenses and managing everyday tasks like doing the laundry and planning transportation. They are finding that life on their own is not always easy, but they try to consider all the factors before making decisions. Luckily, many of these decisions are made easier by using mathematics. Help them stretch their hard-earned dollars to make ends meet.

	skills	completed	grade
2.1	real number operations, comparing numbers		
2.2	real number operations, comparing numbers, algebra		
2.3	rate, time, drawing a diagram, algebra		
2.4	fractions, proportion, number relations, algebra		
2.5	percent, proportion, determining pertinent information		
2.6	discount, percent of decrease		
2.7	schedules, time		
2.8	probability		
2.9	number operations, percent		
2.10	percent of decrease		

Evaluation of work in this unit

_____

_____

_____

_____

_____

2.1 Figuring Out the Furniture

real number operations, comparing numbers
step-by-step

Clever and Smart want furniture for their new house. They are not sure whether they should buy furniture or rent it. The Rent-to-Keep store charges $36 a month for a couch, $16 a month for a coffee table and $28 a month for a chair. If they keep the furniture for 3 years they will own it. Big Buy Furniture sells the same three pieces of furniture. The couch costs $699, the table costs $259, and chair costs $469. If Clever and Smart decide they want to own the furniture, which is the better deal? How much money will they save if they choose the best deal?

☞ Directions

Determine how much money it would cost to rent the furniture for three years and then own it, and how much it would cost to buy it right away. Find the difference in price and state which store offers the best deal. Explain each step you use to get your answer.

1. Determine how many payments will need to be made in three years.

2. Combine all the prices of the Rent-to-Keep items into one price.
Calculate the total cost for three years.

3. Find the total cost of the Big Buy prices.

4. Compare both amounts. Determine which is the better deal.

2.2 Checking and Balancing

real number operations, algebra, comparing numbers
prompted practice

Now that Clever and Smart have built their house, they must pay the monthly bills. They hope to have enough money left over to buy a video game. Use the information on their incomes and expenses to determine if they can buy a game that has a total cost of $52.

Income
Clever earns $608 a month.
Smart earns $30 less than 1.5 times Clever's monthly pay.

Expenses

house payment	$789	water	$56
electricity	$128	gas	$123
telephone	$124	grocery	$212

☞ Directions
Determine how much money Clever and Smart have left after they pay all the monthly bills and decide whether there is enough money to purchase the video game. Explain each step you use.

▸ Calculate the total income of Clever and Smart.

▸ Find the total amount owed in bills.

▸ Find the difference between the two figures and compare the result with the price of the video game.

2.3 Catching the Bus

rate, time, drawing a diagram, algebra
challenge

Name _____

Smart takes the bus to work. Unfortunately, he forgets his lunch at home. Clever grabs the lunch and drives after the bus. The bus has a 15-minute head start and is traveling at an average rate of 40 mph. Clever is traveling at an average rate of 60 mph. How long does Clever take to catch up to the bus? Draw a diagram to solve the problem.

☞ **Directions**

Determine the amount of time it takes Clever to reach the bus. Explain each step you use and why you need that step to solve the problem.

work space   explanation

- -

- -

- -

- -

- -

- -

- -

- -

- -

- -

- -

- -

- -

- -

- -

2.4 Dirty Laundry

fractions, proportion, number relations, algebra
step-by-step

Clever and Smart are doing the laundry. Smart has already done 8 loads. Clever has to do the rest of the loads, which is ⅓ of the laundry. How many loads of laundry are left for her to do?

☞ **Directions**

Determine how many loads of laundry Clever must do. Explain each step you use to solve the problem and the reason for each step. Round your answer to the nearest whole number.

1. Calculate what fraction of the entire job Smart
has already done.

----

2. Set up a proportion where 8 out of an unknown
equals the fraction of completed loads. Use
cross products to set up an algebraic equation.

----

3. Solve for the unknown using inverse operations.

----

4. Find the difference between the total number of
laundry loads and the loads Smart has already
finished. Write your answer in a complete
sentence.

2.5 More Dirty Laundry

percent, proportion, determining pertinent information
prompted practice

Name _____

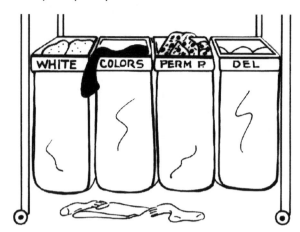

Clever and Smart do 24 loads of laundry a month. Colored clothes make up 50% of the loads. There are half as many white loads as the colored. The remaining loads are permanent press and delicate fabrics. Delicate fabrics make up 12.5% of the laundry. How many loads will it take to do all the colored and the delicate fabrics?

☞ Directions

Determine how many loads of laundry it will take to do both the colored and the delicate fabrics. Round your answer to the nearest whole number. Explain each step, mentioning the numbers and operations that you used.

▶ Find the number of colored loads.

▶ Calculate the number of loads required for the delicate fabrics.

▶ Find the total for colored and delicate loads.

2.6 Mall Madness

discount, percent of decrease
independent practice

It is sale time at the Mite E. Big Shopping Mall. Clever and Smart have found bargains on overalls. Clever found a pair that was originally $43.00 but will be reduced 25% at the register. Smart found a pair that is $43.00 but is reduced 15% and will have an additional 15% taken off the reduced price. Before they decide which type of overalls to buy, they want to find out which price is better.

☞ Directions

Determine the two sale prices and compare them to each other. Explain each step you take to solve the problem and the reason for each step. Use complete sentences to explain your answer.

work space

explanation

2.7 Ticket to Ride

schedules, time
independent practice

Clever and Smart are going to use the mass transportation system to visit the art museum. The first part of the trip will by train. The second part will be by subway. The last part of the journey will be by monorail. Use the schedule to find out when they must leave so that they will arrive at the museum 4 hours before the museum's closing time at 5:00 PM.

- The train ride to the city takes 20 minutes.
- The subway runs every 15 minutes starting at 6:00 AM. It takes 8 minutes to get to the monorail.
- The monorail takes 5 minutes to get to the art museum.

☞ Directions

Using the schedules, determine the time Clever and Smart must take the train to get to the art museum 4 hours before 5:00 PM. Explain each step you use.

Departures	
train	monorail
10:00	11:35
10:45	11:50
11:30	12:05
12:15	12:20
1:00	12:35
1:45	12:55

work space

explanation

- -

- -

- -

- -

- -

- -

- -

- -

- -

- -

- -

- -

- -

- -

2.8 Lots of Lottery Tickets

probability
challenge

Clever is going to take a chance and play the lottery. She figures that if she buys a three-digit lottery ticket, all the possible combinations of numbers will range from 000 to 999. Clever's lucky number is 46. If she plays every number that has the last two digits of 46, what is the probability of one of the numbers being drawn?

☞ Directions

Determine the probability of Clever winning the lottery if she buys only tickets that end in 46. Use complete sentences to explain each step you use to solve the problem and the reason for each step.

work space

explanation

2.9 Food for Thought

number operations, percent
independent practice

Clever and Smart have purchased a dinner theater package that includes two meals and a performance for $45. The dinners alone have a value of $12 each. What percentage of the price is the cost of the theater tickets?

☞ Directions

Determine what percent of $45 is the cost of the theater tickets. Explain each step you use to solve the problem and the reason for each step. Use complete sentences. Round your answer to the nearest whole percent.

work space

explanation

- -

- -

- -

- -

- -

- -

- -

- -

- -

- -

- -

- -

- -

- -

- -

- -

2.10 Wear and Tear

percent of decrease
challenge

Name _____

Clever and Smart use a computer in their home business. The computer was state-of-the-art 3 years ago. It cost $5,400 at that time. Every year, the computer has depreciated (lost value) at a rate of 20% a year. What is the current value of their computer?

☞ Directions

Determine the value of the computer after three years of depreciation. Use complete sentences to explain each step you use to solve the problem and the reason for each step.

work space

explanation

- -

- -

- -

- -

- -

- -

- -

- -

- -

- -

- -

- -

- -

- -

- -

- -

- -

A Well-Deserved Vacation

Clever and Smart are going on a vacation. They need to plan where they will go and how much it will cost to get there. They will encounter a few problems along the way, but they can always use their math skills to help them get back on track. Ride along with them as they plan their travels and figure out their expenses. Stay on track, don't take any detours, and don't get lost.

	skills	completed	grade
3.1	ratio, number operations, problem solving		
3.2	unit price		
3.3	time, rate, drawing a diagram		
3.4	rate, unit price		
3.5	rate, scale, number conversion		
3.6	percent of discount		
3.7	number operations, percent		
3.8	algebra		
3.9	probability		
3.10	similar figures, ratio, proportion		

Evaluation of work in this unit

_____

_____

_____

_____

_____

3.1 Fill'er Up

ratio, number operations, problem solving
step-by-step

Clever and Smart are going on a vacation. They are going to drive to Key Largo, Florida, which is 1312 miles from their home in Mudville, Pennsylvania. They are trying to develop a budget for the trip, and the first thing they need to know is how much gas it will take to drive to Key Largo and back home. They must also calculate how much money all the gasoline will cost. Their car gets 33 miles to the gallon. Gasoline will cost an average of $1.99 per gallon.

☞ Directions

Determine how much money Clever and Smart must budget for the gasoline. Explain each step you use and why you need that step to solve the problem.

1. Determine how many miles they will travel for the entire round trip.

2. Calculate how many gallons of gasoline it will take to travel round trip.

3. Determine the total cost of the gasoline needed to complete the trip.

3.2 Sandwich Assembly Line

unit prices
prompted practice

Name _____

Clever and Smart are making sandwiches for their trip to Key Largo. They are each going to eat 9 sandwiches. They want to know how much each sandwich is going to cost. Look at the list of ingredients and the price list. Use this information to calculate the cost of a single sandwich and the cost of the total number of sandwiches needed for the trip.

one sandwich ingredients	price of ingredients	
2 slices of rye bread	loaf of rye bread (24 slices)	$2.20
1 slice of turkey	turkey (12 slices)	$3.50
1 slice cheese	cheese (12 slices)	$2.70
1 slice tomato	tomato (15 slices)	$1.90
1 piece lettuce	lettuce (30 pieces)	$1.50
1 ounce of mayonnaise	mayonnaise (14 ounces)	$3.40

☞ Directions

Find the cost of a single sandwich and the total cost for all the sandwiches needed for the trip. Round your answer to the nearest cent. Explain the steps you use to find your answer. Label your answer.

▶ Find the unit price of each of the ingredients.

▶ Calculate the cost of a single sandwich.

▶ Determine the total cost of 18 sandwiches.

3.3 Car Trouble

time, rate, drawing a diagram
independent practice

Name _____

Clever and Smart's car begins to overheat while driving to Key Largo. Every 45 miles they have to stop and refill the radiator with water, which takes 12 minutes. The nearest garage is 270 miles away. They call the garage at 8:50 AM to tell them they are coming. If they travel at 60 mph, what time should they tell the mechanic they will arrive at the garage?

☞ Directions

Determine what time Clever and Smart will arrive at the garage. Use complete sentences to explain each step you use and why you need that step to solve the problem.

work space

explanation

- -
- -
- -
- -
- -
- -
- -
- -
- -
- -
- -
- -
- -
- -
- -
- -
- -

3.4 Repair Scare

rate, unit prices
step-by-step

Name _____

Clever and Smart's car needs to have a new thermostat installed. The mechanic at the garage charges $45 an hour. The part costs $24.50. The mechanic takes 2.5 hours to replace the thermostat. What is the total repair bill?

☞ Directions

Determine the total cost to repair Clever and Smart's car. Explain each step you use and why you need that step to solve the problem. Clearly label the result.

1. Calculate the labor cost.

2. Find the total cost of the labor and parts.

3.5 Middle of Nowhere

rate, scale, number conversion
prompted practice

Clever and Smart take a wrong turn. They end up in the Middle of Nowhere. Use the map to determine the distance to Next Town. Then, calculate how long it will take them to get to Next Town if they travel at an average speed of 55 mph. Round your answer to the nearest tenth and convert your answer to hours and minutes.

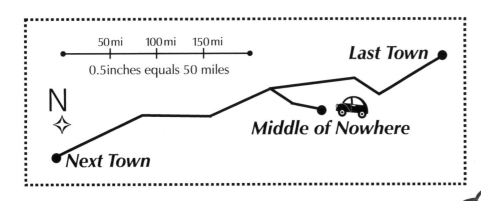

☞ Directions

Determine the time it will take Clever and Smart to get from the Middle of Nowhere to Next Town. Explain each step you use and why you need that step to solve the problem.

▸ Find the total distance in inches. Convert your answer into miles.

```
- - - - - - - - - - - - - - - - - - -
- - - - - - - - - - - - - - - - - - -
- - - - - - - - - - - - - - - - - - -
```

▸ Calculate the amount of time it takes to travel the distance. You may need to use the distance formula: rate x time = distance.

```
- - - - - - - - - - - - - - - - - - -
- - - - - - - - - - - - - - - - - - -
- - - - - - - - - - - - - - - - - - -
```

3.6 Hotel at Last

percent of discount
independent practice

Name _____

Clever and Smart use the Internet to reserve their hotel room. In addition to a 25% discount for advanced reservations, they receive a 10% for using the Internet. They plan to stay five nights. The original hotel room price is $169 per night. With their discounts, how much is the cost of their entire stay?

☞ Directions

Determine the total cost of five nights at the hotel. Use complete sentences to explain each step you use and why you need that step to solve the problem. Write your final answer in a complete sentence.

Note: The discounts are not taken separately (25% of the room price and then 10% of the discounted price) but are combined for one total discount.

work space

explanation

_ _

_ _

_ _

_ _

_ _

_ _

_ _

_ _

_ _

_ _

_ _

_ _

_ _

_ _

_ _

_ _

3.7 Dining Out

number operations, percent
independent practice

Name _____

Clever and Smart decide to treat themselves to a
dinner at the Upscale Restaurant. Clever's meal costs
$23, while Smart's meal costs $26. Their appetizer
before the meal costs $8. Clever and Smart each have
a drink costing $3.50 apiece. The service is
outstanding, so they want to leave a 20% tip. How
much money altogether should they leave for the
meals and tip?

☞ **Directions**

Determine how much money Clever and Smart should give the server for their meals and a 20% tip.
Explain each step you use and why you need that step to solve the problem. Write your final answer
in a complete sentence.

work space   explanation

_____

_____

_____

_____

_____

_____

_____

_____

_____

_____

_____

_____

_____

_____

_____

_____

3.8 Amusements at the Park

algebra
challenge

Clever and Smart go to the Happy Dog Amusement Park. There are two types of tickets sold at the park:
- all-day ride ticket $25.00
- ride and dog show combo $35.00

The ticket takers are a little lazy on their jobs. When the park manager does the books at the close of the day, there is no record of the number of each type of ticket sold. All the manager has is the total number of people in the park and the total amount of money collected. There were 4,903 visitors, and the total sales were $155,155.00. How many tickets of each type were purchased?

☞ Directions

Determine how many of each type of ticket were purchased. Write your answer in complete sentences, explaining each step you use and why you need that step to solve the problem.

work space   explanation

3.9 Bungle in the Jungle

probability
independent practice

Name _____

Clever and Smart are visiting Safari Adventure, but they have lost their guide book. They know that there are 5 lions, 10 zebras, 6 elephants, 4 hippopotamuses, and 1 rhinoceros. If all factors are equal, what is the probability that the next two animals they see will be a hippopotamus and a zebra?

☞ Directions

Determine the probability that the next two animals they see will be a hippopotamus and a zebra. Explain each step you use and why you need that step to solve the problem. Write your final answer in a complete sentence.

work space   explanation

3.10 Roadside Attraction

similar figures, ratio, proportion
independent practice

Name _____

Clever and Smart stop at a roadside attraction, a house shaped like a cheese wedge. They buy a scale model of the house. The original house is 24 feet in height. The model has a height of 6 inches and has a length of 8 inches. What is the length of the actual house?

☞ Directions

Determine the length of the actual cheese wedge house. Explain each step you use and why you need that step to solve the problem. Write your final answer in a complete sentence.

work space

explanation

--- --- --- --- --- --- --- --- --- --- --- --- --- ---

--- --- --- --- --- --- --- --- --- --- --- --- --- ---

--- --- --- --- --- --- --- --- --- --- --- --- --- ---

--- --- --- --- --- --- --- --- --- --- --- --- --- ---

--- --- --- --- --- --- --- --- --- --- --- --- --- ---

--- --- --- --- --- --- --- --- --- --- --- --- --- ---

--- --- --- --- --- --- --- --- --- --- --- --- --- ---

--- --- --- --- --- --- --- --- --- --- --- --- --- ---

--- --- --- --- --- --- --- --- --- --- --- --- --- ---

--- --- --- --- --- --- --- --- --- --- --- --- --- ---

--- --- --- --- --- --- --- --- --- --- --- --- --- ---

--- --- --- --- --- --- --- --- --- --- --- --- --- ---

--- --- --- --- --- --- --- --- --- --- --- --- --- ---

--- --- --- --- --- --- --- --- --- --- --- --- --- ---

--- --- --- --- --- --- --- --- --- --- --- --- --- ---

--- --- --- --- --- --- --- --- --- --- --- --- --- ---

Care and Feeding

Clever and Smart found a puppy, and after unsuccessfully trying to locate its owner, they decided to keep the dog. Owning a pet means new responsibilities and lots of bills. Using math, they are able to get the best price on dog food, build a fence for the dog, keep track of the dog's growth, and, of course, pay the veterinary bill.

	skills	completed	grade
4.1	unit price		
4.2	unit price, comparing real numbers		
4.3	unit price, comparing real numbers		
4.4	measure of central tendency		
4.5	finding a pattern, marking a graph, extrapolating		
4.6	percent, number operations		
4.7	permutations, combinations		
4.8	perimeter, measurement, number operations		
4.9	surface area		
4.10	time, rate, unit price, projected cost		

Evaluation of work in this unit

_____

_____

_____

_____

_____

4.1 Lost and Found

unit price
step-by-step

Name _____

Clever and Smart have found a lost puppy. They are going to place an advertisement in the lost and found section of the local paper. The advertisement contains 55 words and costs $25.00. The first 25 words cost $10. What is the cost per word for the remaining words in the ad?

☞ Directions

Determine the unit cost of a single word in the advertisement. Use complete sentences to explain each step you use and why you need that step to solve the problem. Clearly label your solution.

1. Find out how many words in excess of 25 are in the advertisement.

_ _

_ _

2. Find out how much over $10 the advertisement cost.

_ _

_ _

3. Divide the cost of the excess words by the number of words to find the cost per word.

_ _

_ _

_ _

4.2 It's in the Bag

unit price, comparing real numbers
prompted practice

Clever and Smart had no response to their lost and found advertisement, so they are keeping the puppy they found. They each buy a bag of dog food. Clever buys a 25-pound bag for $8.99. Smart spends $2.99 on a smaller, 5-pound bag. Who gets the better deal and what is the difference in the price per pound of the two bags?

☞ Directions

Determine the unit cost of a single pound of each kind of dog food and compare the two prices to find the best price. Use complete sentences to explain how you got your answer.

▸ Determine the unit price for a pound of each kind of dog food.

▸ Compare the two unit prices. Find the difference between the higher and lower-priced dog food.

▸ Write a sentence telling which is the best deal and how much cheaper it was per pound.

4.3 Doing the Can Can

unit price, comparing real numbers
independent practice

Name _____

Clever and Smart want to vary the diet of their new puppy. They each buy cans of a special diet dog food. Clever buys 14 cans of dog food for $11.89. Smart buys 5 cans of the dog food for $3.89. They want to know who gets the better deal.

☞ Directions

Determine the better price by comparing unit prices per can. Explain each step you use and why you need that step to solve the problem. Write your final answer in a complete sentence.

work space   explanation

- -
- -
- -
- -
- -
- -
- -
- -
- -
- -
- -
- -
- -
- -
- -
- -
- -

4.4 Walking the Dog

measure of central tendency
step-by-step

Name _____

Clever and Smart each take turns walking the puppy. Clever walks the puppy in the morning. Last week she walked it 0.75 miles on Monday and 0.65 miles on Tuesday, Wednesday and Thursday. On Friday she walked the puppy only 0.5 mile. She walked the puppy 1.2 miles on Saturday and 1.8 miles on Sunday. What is the average distance Clever walked the puppy during the week?

☞ Directions

Determine the average distance walked for the seven days. Explain each step you use and why you need that step to solve the problem. Write your final answer in a complete sentence.

1. Find the total number of miles walked during the week.

_ _

_ _

_ _

2. Divide the total number of miles by the number of days in the week. Round your answer to the nearest hundredth of a mile and clearly label it.

_ _

_ _

_ _

4.5 How Big Will It Get?

*finding a pattern, making a graph, extrapolating
prompted practice*

Name _____

The puppy seems to grow and grow. Clever and Smart want to make a weekly growth chart. They have gathered information for the past seven weeks. Use their information to create a growth chart. Then predict what the puppy's weight will be at the end of ten weeks.

Week	Weight
1	22 lbs
2	25 lbs
3	28 lbs
4	31 lbs
5	34 lbs
6	37 lbs
7	40 lbs

☞ Directions

Create a chart for the first seven weeks of the puppy's weight. Predict the next three weeks of growth for the puppy and its weight after the tenth week. Write your answer in a complete sentence.

▸ Label the two axes of the graph.

▸ Plot the points for the first seven weeks of growth.

▸ Find the pattern.

▸ Using the pattern, plot the last three weeks of growth and state the puppy's weight in the last week.

- -

- -

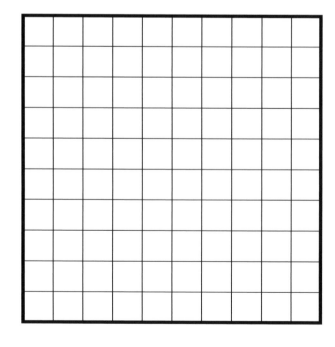

46

4.6 Vet Bills and Budget Chills

percent, number operations
independent practice

Name _____

With the addition of a new member to their household, Clever and Smart have to add the veterinary bill to their budget. A yearly check up costs $60, and yearly vaccinations cost $135. The monthly heartworm medicine is $15. If their yearly budget for extra expenses is $1,250, what percent of the budget are the vet bills?

☞ Directions

Determine what percent of the yearly budget should be allotted for veterinary bills. Round your answer to the nearest hundredth. Use complete sentences to explain each step you use and why you need that step to solve the problem.

work space

explanation

4.7 The Dog Show You Know

permutations, combinations
independent practice

Name _____

At the annual Greenhills Dog Show there are four
different classes of dogs. There are the toy, sporting,
working dog, and herding classes. This year's show has
6 different breeds of toy class dogs. There are 10
different breeds of dogs in the sporting class. The
working dog class has 8 different dogs, and the
herding class has 5 different types of dogs. Each class
will have a winner for best of the class. How many
combinations of winning dogs are possible?

☞ Directions

Determine the total number of combinations of the winners that can be created from the four classes
of dogs. Clearly explain each step you use. Write your final answer in a complete sentence.

work space

explanation

- -
- -
- -
- -
- -
- -
- -
- -
- -
- -
- -
- -
- -
- -

4.8 Don't Fence Me In

Name _____

perimeter, measurement, number operations
independent practice

Clever and Smart are putting up a fence around their property to keep the puppy safe. The fence they want to buy costs $1.95 per foot. Each pole they use costs $5.45. They will need a pole every 5 feet. Use the diagram to find the total cost of the fencing project.

☞ **Directions**
Determine the cost of fencing for the entire yard. Include both the cost of the fence and the posts. Explain each step you use and why you need that step to solve the problem. Write your explanations in complete sentences.

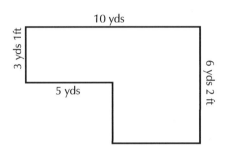

work space

explanation

_____
_____
_____
_____
_____
_____
_____
_____
_____
_____
_____
_____
_____
_____
_____
_____

4.9 Gear Is Here

surface area
challenge

Clever and Smart want to build a storage box for the puppy's food and gear. They are building it in the shape of a rectangular prism. The sides will have the length of 4′ and a height of 3′. The top and the floor will measure 4′ by 4′. They are going to coat the entire exterior of the box with a weather-resistant covering. The weather covering costs $1.25 a square foot. They need to know the total surface area of the storage box and the total cost for the all weather covering.

☞ **Directions**

Determine the total surface area of the storage box and the cost of the all-weather covering. Explain each step you use and why you need that step to solve the problem.

work space   explanation

__ __ __ __ __ __ __ __ __ __ __ __ __

__ __ __ __ __ __ __ __ __ __ __ __ __

__ __ __ __ __ __ __ __ __ __ __ __ __

__ __ __ __ __ __ __ __ __ __ __ __ __

__ __ __ __ __ __ __ __ __ __ __ __ __

__ __ __ __ __ __ __ __ __ __ __ __ __

__ __ __ __ __ __ __ __ __ __ __ __ __

__ __ __ __ __ __ __ __ __ __ __ __ __

__ __ __ __ __ __ __ __ __ __ __ __ __

__ __ __ __ __ __ __ __ __ __ __ __ __

__ __ __ __ __ __ __ __ __ __ __ __ __

__ __ __ __ __ __ __ __ __ __ __ __ __

__ __ __ __ __ __ __ __ __ __ __ __ __

__ __ __ __ __ __ __ __ __ __ __ __ __

4.10 How Much Does It Eat

time, rate, unit price, projected cost
challenge

The puppy has grown into a sizable dog with a sizeable appetite. Clever and Smart are calculating how much it will cost to feed the dog for a year. The dog eats one can of dog food each day and consumes a bag of dry dog food each week. The canned food sells for $2.37 for three cans, and the bags cost $7.98 each. How much will it cost to feed the dog for a year?

☞ **Directions**

Determine the annual cost to feed the dog. Explain each step you use and why you need that step to solve the problem. Write your explanation in complete sentences.

work space

explanation

Minding a Business

Clever and Smart are starting a business. They not only have to set up their manufacturing facility, but they also have to deal with paying their employees. All these tasks involve mathematical calculations. Sharpen your pencil and help them turn their business venture into a success.

	skills	completed	grade
5.1	units of time and labor costs, multi-step problem solving		
5.2	creating and applying formulas, using new information		
5.3	Pythagorean formula, number operations		
5.4	Pythagorean formula, operations with variables, operation order		
5.5	Pythagorean formula, operations with variables		
5.6	Pythagorean formula, multi-step problem		
5.7	measurement, circumference, number operations		
5.8	measurement, circumference, completing a chart		
5.9	volume of a cylinder		
5.10	using a table, applying information, multi-step problem solving		

Evaluation of work in this unit

_____

_____

_____

_____

_____

5.1 Time and Time Again

Name _____

units of time and labor cost, multi-step problem solving
independent practice

Clever and Smart are preparing to open their first business. It is a factory that will produce environmentally-friendly automobiles. They are going to hire 5 workers to build the cars. Each worker will be paid $12 an hour. They are also going to hire 3 people to work as a cleaning and maintenance crew for $9 an hour. Each employee will be scheduled to work 40 hours a week. It will be 18 weeks before they see the first payments for the automobiles they produce. How much cash on hand must they have to pay their workers for 18 weeks?

☞ Directions

Find the total labor costs for all their employees for 18 weeks. Explain all the steps you take and the mathematical concepts you use to solve the problem. Write your final answer in a complete sentence.

work area

explanation

(blank writing lines)

5.2 Laboring Over Cost

creating and applying formulas, using new information
independent practice

Name _____

Clever and Smart have an assembly line that produces one car every 3 days. Their factory operates 6 days a week with 5 workers who work 8 hours a day. They pay each worker $12 an hour for the first 40 hours and 1.5 times that amount for every hour over 40 in a one-week pay period. They have orders for 20 cars. How much money must they pay their workers all together to complete all the orders?

☞ Directions
Find the total labor cost for building 20 cars. Explain all the steps you take and the mathematical concepts you use to solve the problem. Write your final answer in a complete sentence.

work area

explanation

5.3 Triangle Tangle

Pythagorean formula, number operations
step-by-step

Name _____

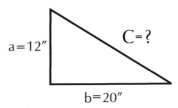

Clever and Smart are installing the side windows on their car. They want to put a rain guard on them. They want to know the length of rain guard needed to complete their project. They know it will be equal to the length of the longest side of the triangle-shaped window. This side is known as the hypotenuse. They have the measurements for the other two shorter sides. Help them find the length of the missing side.

☞ Directions
Use the diagram to help you solve the problem. Find the length of the unknown side. Write your final answer in a complete sentence.

1. Recall the Pythagorean formula.

$$\sqrt{a^2 + b^2} = c$$

2. Find the square of side a.

3. Find the square of side b.

4. Find the sum of the squares of sides a and b.

5. Find the square root of the sum of the squares of sides a and b. This is the length of the rain guard.

5.4 Ramp Champ

Pythagorean formula, operations with variables, order of operation prompted practice

Name _____

Clever and Smart are building a ramp to load and unload the trucks that come to their factory. The ramp has to be 3 feet high at the side that touches the truck and 8 feet long. They want to know the length of the board needed to make the floor of the ramp. Round your answer to the nearest tenth.

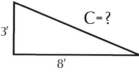

☞ **Directions**

Use the diagram to help you solve the problem. Find the length of the unknown side. In complete sentences, explain all the steps you take and mathematical concepts you use to solve the problem.

▸ Recall the Pythagorean theorem.

‒ ‒ ‒ ‒ ‒ ‒ ‒ ‒ ‒ ‒ ‒ ‒ ‒ ‒ ‒ ‒ ‒ ‒ ‒
‒ ‒ ‒ ‒ ‒ ‒ ‒ ‒ ‒ ‒ ‒ ‒ ‒ ‒ ‒ ‒ ‒ ‒ ‒

▸ Find the squares of sides a and b.

‒ ‒ ‒ ‒ ‒ ‒ ‒ ‒ ‒ ‒ ‒ ‒ ‒ ‒ ‒ ‒ ‒ ‒ ‒
‒ ‒ ‒ ‒ ‒ ‒ ‒ ‒ ‒ ‒ ‒ ‒ ‒ ‒ ‒ ‒ ‒ ‒ ‒

▸ Find the sum of the squares.

‒ ‒ ‒ ‒ ‒ ‒ ‒ ‒ ‒ ‒ ‒ ‒ ‒ ‒ ‒ ‒ ‒ ‒ ‒
‒ ‒ ‒ ‒ ‒ ‒ ‒ ‒ ‒ ‒ ‒ ‒ ‒ ‒ ‒ ‒ ‒ ‒ ‒

▸ Find the square root of the sum of the squares.

‒ ‒ ‒ ‒ ‒ ‒ ‒ ‒ ‒ ‒ ‒ ‒ ‒ ‒ ‒ ‒ ‒ ‒ ‒
‒ ‒ ‒ ‒ ‒ ‒ ‒ ‒ ‒ ‒ ‒ ‒ ‒ ‒ ‒ ‒ ‒ ‒ ‒

5.5 Dawning of the Awning

Pythagorean formula, operations with variables
independent practice

Clever and Smart are installing an awning. The diagonal
side (hypotenuse) of the awning is 10 feet long. The
shortest side is 5 feet in length. They want to attach a rod
from the wall to the bottom end of the awning. They need
to know how long the rod must be. Find the missing length
of the rod.

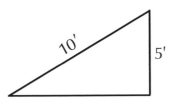

☞ Directions

Use the diagram to help you solve the problem. Find the length of the rod. Explain all the steps you
take and the mathematical concepts you use to solve the problem. Round your answer to the nearest
tenth. Write your final answer in a complete sentence.

work area   explanation

5.6 Moving Belts and Improving Belts

Pythagorean formula, multi-step problem challenge

Name _____

Clever and Smart want to upgrade their current conveyor belt system. To do this, they need to figure out how much belt material they need. The system sits on a 3-foot-high platform and moves cargo to the second floor, 12 feet above the ground floor. The platform that the conveyor system sits on is 15 feet long. The belt forms one continuous loop. In order for the belt to fit around the drive wheels, they need to order an additional foot of belt material (6" for each end). Determine the total length of belt they will need for the top and bottom of the conveyor loop plus extra for the wheels on each end.

9'

3'

15'

☞ Directions

Find the total length of the conveyor belt. Round your answer to the nearest tenth. Using complete sentences, explain all the steps you take and the mathematical concepts you use to solve the problem.

work area

explanation

_____

_____

_____

_____

_____

_____

_____

_____

_____

_____

_____

_____

_____

_____

5.7 As the Tire Turns

measurement, circumference, number operations
prompted practice

Name _____

Clever and Smart are designing a new car. They are thinking about using 15-inch diameter tires on their car. They want to know how many rotations a 15-inch tire will make every mile.

1 mile = 5,280 feet
$C = \pi d$
$\pi = 3.14$

☞ Directions

Determine how many rotations a tire will make every mile. Round your answer to the nearest whole number. Explain all the steps you take and the mathematical concepts you use to solve the problem. Write your final answer in a complete sentence.

▶ Find the circumference of the tire.

▶ Convert the circumference to feet.

▶ Divide the number of feet in a mile by the number of feet in the circumference of the tire. Each time the tire travels the length of its circumference, it equals one rotation.

5.8 Tired of Tires

measurement, circumference, completing a chart
independent practice

Name _____

Clever and Smart are selecting tire sizes for their car. They cannot decide whether to install 13-inch or 14-inch diameter tires. The circumference determines how many times the wheel turns in a mile. Clever and Smart want to see a chart comparing the diameters of the two tires, their circumferences, and the number of rotations per mile.

☞ Directions

Complete this chart. Explain all the steps you take and the mathematical concepts you use to solve the problem. Round your answer to the nearest tenth. Write your final answer in a complete sentence.

	diameter	circumference	rotations per mile
tire A			
tire B			
difference			

work space

explanation

- -
- -
- -
- -
- -
- -
- -
- -
- -
- -
- -
- -
- -

5.9 Thanks for the Water Tanks

volume of a cylinder
challenge

Name _____

Clever and Smart are going to build a hot water tank. They are debating what size to make the tank. They want to use a single piece of sheet metal to make the outside casing of the tank. The piece of sheet metal has the dimensions of 8.5 feet by 11 feet. The sheet can be used to make a water tank that is 8.5 feet tall with an 11-foot circumference or it can make a tank 11 feet tall with an 8.5-foot circumference. Which tank will hold more water or will they both hold the same?

$$C = \pi \cdot d \qquad b = \pi \cdot r^2$$
$$V = b \cdot h \qquad \text{use } \pi = 3.14$$

☞ Directions

Find the dimensions of the water tank that will hold the most water or prove that both ways will hold the same amount of water. Use complete sentences to explain all the steps you take and the mathematical concepts you use to solve the problem.

work area   explanation

5.10 Bang for the Banquet

using a table, applying information, multi-step problem solving
independent practice

Name _____

After a year of manufacturing environmentally-friendly automobiles, Clever and Smart want to reward their employees. They are going to have a banquet for all their workers. They need to find the total cost for the banquet. Use the following information to calculate the price of having the banquet.

table rental	$8.00 per table (each table seats 6 people)
place settings	$4.50 per person
food	roast beef dinner = $15.00
	turkey dinner = $14.50

food orders	
first shift	second shift
8 beef	5 beef
4 turkey	7 turkey

☞ **Directions**

Find the total cost the banquet. Explain all the steps you take and write your final answer in a complete sentence.

Hint: Use the food orders to find out the number of employees that will be at the banquet.

work space   explanation

Home Sweet Home

Welcome to Clever and Smart's home. In this unit you will help them with some of the situations they encounter in everyday life. Whether saving money, preparing a holiday meal, or buying furniture, Clever and Smart want to make the best decision. Join in and help these two happy homeowners with their calculations.

	skills	completed	grade
6.1	algebra, interest		
6.2	simple interest, algebra		
6.3	real number operations		
6.4	time, units of measure conversion		
6.5	rate, distance, algebra, comparing numbers		
6.6	schedules, time		
6.7	algebra, number operations		
6.8	geometric formulas, number operations		
6.9	geometric formulas, percent, comparing real numbers		
6.10	percent, operations with decimals		

Evaluation of work in this unit

_____

_____

_____

_____

_____

6.1 Holiday Savings

algebra, interest
step-by-step

Clever and Smart started a holiday savings plan. They deposited $500 in the plan at the beginning of the year and received a Smart rate of interest of 5%. They also deposited $15 a week all year long. In addition to the interest, the bank added $26 more to their account at the end of the year. How much money did Clever and Smart have in their account at the end of the year?

☞ Directions

Determine the total amount of money Clever and Smart have in their savings account at the end of the year. Explain each step you use and why you need that step to solve the problem. Write your final answer in a complete sentence.

1. Use the simple interest formula (I = p·r·t) to calculate interest on $500.

----

2. Find the total of interest and principle.

----

3. Find the product of weeks in a year and the amount deposited each week.

----

4. Find the sum of weekly deposits, interest, principle, and money the bank adds to the account.

6.2 Saving for a Rainy Day

simple interest, algebra
prompted practice

Name _____

Clever and Smart start a savings account. They deposit $10,000 in it. They promise to keep the money in the bank for 5 years. After the end of the 5 years they will receive 7% interest for each year. What will be the total amount they will have in the account after 5 years?

☞ Directions
Determine the total amount of money that will be in the savings account (principle and interest) after 5 years. Explain each step you use and why you need that step to solve the problem. Clearly label your answer.

▶ Recall the formula for finding simple interest.

▶ Convert the annual percentage rate into a decimal.

▶ Use the formula and substitute the values for principle and rate to calculate interest.

▶ Add interest to principle to get the total amount in the account.

6.3 Stocking Stuffers

real number operations
independent practice

Clever and Smart are going to donate holiday gifts to the children's center. They want to buy each child a small gift and some candy and put them into a stocking. The stockings cost $1.25. The gifts cost $3.75, and the candy costs $1.75 for each stocking. There are 48 kids at the center. How much will it cost them to provide one filled stocking for each of the 48 children?

☞ **Directions**

Determine the total cost of the holiday stockings, gifts, and candy. Using complete sentences, explain each step you use and why you need that step to solve the problem.

workspace   explanation

_____

_____

_____

_____

_____

_____

_____

_____

_____

_____

_____

_____

_____

_____

_____

_____

6.4 The Big Bird

time, units of measure conversion
step-by-step

Name _____

Clever and Smart are planning their holiday feast. They will be serving a turkey dinner at the homeless shelter. They purchase the largest bird they can find. It weighs 28 pounds. Dinner will be served at 12:30 PM.
• It takes 13 minutes per pound to cook the turkey at 350°.
• The turkey will need to sit out of the oven and cool for 1 hour and 15 minutes, before it can be sliced and served. What time will Clever and Smart have to put the turkey into the oven so that it will be ready at dinnertime?

☞ **Directions**
Determine what time Clever will have to put the turkey into the oven so dinner can be served at 12:30 PM. Explain each step you take and why you use that step to solve the problem. Clearly label your answer.

1. Calculate how many minutes it will take to cook the turkey.

     -
     -

2. Convert the minutes into hours and minutes.

     -
     -

3. Find the total time needed to cook the turkey and allow it to cool.

     -
     -

4. Work backwards to determine the time when the turkey needs to be put in the oven.

     -
     -
     -

6.5 Bus Fuss

rate, distance, algebra, comparing numbers
prompted practice

Name _____

Clever and Smart are taking the bus to the shopping mall. Smart wants to buy a surprise birthday gift for Clever. He will need to get to the mall ahead of her. There are two different buses to the mall, the express and the limited. The express bus travels non-stop 20 miles to the mall at a rate of 45 mph. The limited travels at 35 mph and makes three 5-minute stops to pick up passengers. Both buses leave at the same time. If Smart takes the express and Clever takes the limited, how much time will Smart have to shop for the surprise gift?

☞ Directions

Determine how much time Smart has to shop if he takes the express bus and Clever takes the limited. Explain each step you use and why you need that step to solve the problem. Round your answer to the nearest minute. Write your final answer in a complete sentence.

▸ Recall the distance formula.

rate x time = distance

▸ Substitute the values for each bus and solve for the time.

_____

_____

▸ Add the time for the stops to the time for the limited bus.

_____

_____

▸ Find the difference between the times for the two buses.

_____

_____

_____

6.6 Buses and Trains

schedules, time
independent practice

Name _____

Clever and Smart are going to travel to a convention.
They will take a bus from their town to the city, where
they will catch the train to the convention. Use the
schedules to determine how long it will take them to
get to the convention. Do not include any layover
time in your final answer.

Bus Schedule
The bus leaves at 10:20 AM and arrives in the city at 1:10 PM.

Train Schedule
The train leaves at 2:45 PM and arrives at the convention at 5:30 PM.

☞ Directions

Use the schedules to determine the total amount of time it will take Clever and Smart to travel to the
convention. Explain each step you use and why you need that step to solve the problem. Write your
final answer in a complete sentence.

work space   explanation

- -

- -

- -

- -

- -

- -

- -

- -

- -

- -

- -

- -

- -

- -

6.7 Furnishing a Room

algebra, number operations
independent practice

Name _____

Clever and Smart have purchased a 5-piece dining room set. They put $250 down at the time of purchase and are going to pay $65 a month for the next 3 years. The set sells for $1,540. How much are they paying in interest?

☞ **Directions**

Determine the amount of interest paid on the dining room set. In complete sentences, explain each step you use and why you need that step to solve the problem.

work space

explanation

_____
_____
_____
_____
_____
_____
_____
_____
_____
_____
_____
_____
_____
_____
_____
_____
_____
_____
_____
_____